KV-684-920

Contents

What Should She Do?

Henry VIII is famous for having six wives. He divorced two and executed two. One outlived him and one, Jane Seymour, died bearing him the son and heir he craved. At the time of this story Jane didn't know the King would execute Anne Boleyn and that he would marry Jane herself. All she knew was that he wanted her as his mistress and she had a hard choice to make.

The purse in my lap is heavy with gold sovereigns – there must be a fortune. As for the letter I know what's in it even though I haven't opened it yet. Both are from King Henry, whose attentions towards me are becoming more and more obvious. It's clear he wants me as his next mistress. How did I, Jane Seymour, ever get into this situation?

I've known for a long time that the King has mistresses. By the time I became a lady-in-waiting to his wife, Queen Catharine of Aragon, the King's relationship with Anne Boleyn was the talk of the whole country, not just the Court. Even the people in our village in Wiltshire gossiped about it.

'Well, after all, that Catharine is old enough to be his mother.''

'And she's not given him a son, that must go hard with him.'

'Yes, just a daughter and a string of dead babies. He must feel that God's punishing him for marrying her in the first place, and her his brother's wife!'

'Punishment be damned! It's not God he's thinking about, not by a long way! He's always had a mistress on the side, the Boleyn girl's just a bit smarter than the rest, that's all. She's keeping him dangling, to see just how far she can get!'

'Well Miss Jane will need to look out, and her about to go to Court and all!'

'She's no need to worry! She's a nice little thing, but she's no beauty, is she? And too quiet and too clever by half! The King likes a pretty face and an empty head, so I've heard, and she's got neither!'

Tudors and Stuarts

ROSEMARY REES
JANE SHUTER

Reed Educational and Professional Publishing Ltd Halley Court, Jordan Hill, Oxford
OX2 8EJ

MELBOURNE AUCKLAND OXFORD CHICAGO PORTSMOUTH NH IBADAN
GABORONE JOHANNESBURG

Heinemann is a registered trademark of Reed Educational and Professional
Publishing Ltd.

First published 1998

02   01   00
10 9 8 7 6 5 4 3 2

British Library Cataloguing in Publication Data is available from the British Library
on request

ISBN 0435 32262 1

Produced by Magnet Harlequin, Oxford

Illustrated by Stephen Wisdom

Printed in Scotland by Scotprint

Acknowledgements

Adaptations and extracts from the following are by kind permission of the copyright
holders:

Terry Deary, *The Truth about Guy Fawkes*, first published in the UK by Franklin
Watts, a division of the Watts Publishing Group.
Leon Garfield, *The Sound of Coaches*, Kestrel.
Alfred Noyes, *The Highwayman,* by permission of Hugh Noyes on behalf of the
Alfred Noyes literary estate.
Mary Rhind, *The Dark Shadow*, Canongate Books.
Rosemary Sutcliff, *Simon,* Oxford University Press.
Henry Treece, *Wickham and the Armada*, Hulton Press.
Barbara Willard, *The Grove of Green Holly,* Constable Young Books.

942.05

I wasn't hurt by the remark. It was obviously true. No one took any notice of me when I went to Court .

The King only had eyes for Anne Boleyn, who behaved as if she was the queen. The Queen herself was constantly ignored and insulted by Henry, and had become withdrawn, keeping mostly to herself. As one of her ladies, I also existed in a way that was a part of the Court yet separate from it.

Then there was turmoil. Anne became pregnant. The King moved fast. He divorced the Queen and married Anne.

Anne chose me as one of her ladies-in-waiting. 'The plainer the better!' she remarked.

The baby was born. It was a girl. Henry had pinned his hopes on it being a boy, an heir to the throne. He showed his displeasure by not going to the christening. But Anne won him round. She was, after all, young and strong. 'I'll have plenty more babies yet, daughters and sons!' she announced.

But by now the King was seeking a new interest. 'Once he has won a woman she's no longer of interest to him,' one of Anne's ladies said to me. 'He's already tried to kiss me, and more.'

'He's one of those men who likes a wife to have the babies and a mistress to have fun with,' said another. 'There are plenty like that. But Queen Anne's not likely to sit around having babies and quietly sewing while he enjoys himself!'

'Well, she needs to be careful. If she's unfaithful, who knows what will happen? He expects an obedient wife. And he expects a son, fast. She wants to concentrate on that.' But Queen Anne did take lovers.

Then in autumn 1535 two things happened. The Queen was pregnant again and King Henry came to Wiltshire for the hunting and stayed at our family home as a guest. I helped to organise the entertainments. It was now that the King noticed me. He made advances but I pretended not to notice and did all I could to indicate that I was a modest young woman and not given to flirting. But this made him pursue me more. Back at Court, he began giving me presents and insisting that I danced with him. We also sat and talked, him telling me how sick he was of empty-headed chatter and how he welcomed serious conversations on serious subjects.

The Queen noticed. Of course she did. I don't know what she said to the King, but she certainly ranted at me. 'Do you think you can take my husband from me!' she shrieked. 'I'm not taken in by your little ways! Pretending to be shy, pretending to be reluctant to accept his presents, his advances, do you think I do not see through your tricks?'

'Madam, I swear I do not wish to encourage the King. He is your husband. I…'

'Yes, he is my husband, and so he will stay! Don't think otherwise! I will not have you about me anymore – get out!'

Anne's supporters did all they could to blacken my name. When Anne miscarried they said it was caused by her jealousy of me, and they said that the baby was a boy.

All the plotting and scheming made me quite ill. My family were also drawn into the affair, urging me not to insult the King by refusing him, suggesting that I should give in to him for the sake of the family, suggesting that I should insist that he marry me and divorce Anne… the suggestions were endless, the pressure on me, from both sides, was great. So I escaped to Greenwich, to get away from the Court. The Queen cannot bear me near her and the King cannot bear me not to be near him.

What shall I do? I'm sure his letter asks me to be his mistress. If I refuse him, I don't know what he'll do. He has a ferocious temper, I've seen it. He could ruin my family. But can I become his mistress? What about my honour? If he then got rid of me, who would marry me? I have been urged to become his mistress, get pregnant, and then he might marry me. But Anne did that and it hasn't brought her happiness or peace. I never wanted to be at the centre of such a storm. Now all I want is to be out of it, with as little harm as possible. Sir Nicholas Carew has just been to see me, with yet more schemes.

'Think on this, Jane,' he urged. 'The King wants you and he will either have you or ruin you. I know him well. That is the way his mind works. This is the point when your power is strongest. This is the point where you can ask the most. So it is now that you must demand he divorces Anne and marries you. He's divorced once for the sake of a son, he'll do it again.'

I must reply today. I have to decide, now. But what shall I do?

A Tale of Two Abbots

**The life of Fountains Abbey came to an abrupt end on 26 November 1539 when its wealth was seized to satisfy Henry VIII's need for money and his desire to rid the country of the influence of the Catholic Church.
This story is told by an old monk remembering those days at the Abbey.**

I finished tapping the barrel. The claret was good and would go well on Father Abbot's table when he had guests. Or even when he didn't. I was well satisfied. I stood and stretched, breathing in the cool air of the Cellarium. Time to lock up and prepare for vespers in the great Abbey church. I was crossing the cloister, head bowed, sandals flip-flopping on the warm stone, when, 'Brother Benedict, Brother Benedict. Wait! Wait!' I stopped in my tracks. Shouting? In the cloister? Round the corner hurtled little Brother Paul, all ginger hair and freckles, his tonsure not yet cut, his vows not yet taken. What was the novice-master thinking of, allowing this kind of behaviour? Paul skidded to a halt in front of me. I was ready to be severe with the boy. These young novices have to learn respect, and silence and... but the boy interrupted my thoughts.

'I beg your forgiveness, Brother Benedict, but I have a message from Father Abbot. He asks that you attend him in the Chapter House at once.'

I looked at him in amazement, all thought of correcting his behaviour gone. For Abbot William Thirsk to send a message with a novice, and a message that implied we would both miss vespers, meant that something of unforeseen urgency had occurred.

Father Abbot was waiting for me. 'Brother Benedict, we have trouble almost at our gates. I have just had word that our affairs are to be investigated by two of Cromwell's men, Richard Leyton and Thomas Leigh. They have already left St Mary's Abbey in York and will be here soon. Will you alert Brother Stephen, the guestmaster? And will you make sure that your books and accounts are all in order? The Prior and I will have all documents relating to the running of the Abbey gathered together and in good order by the morning.'

He looked older and greyer than I had ever seen him. Suddenly he raised his head and looked me straight in the eyes. 'Benedict, I am a marked man. You remember when Sir Thomas Manners tried to get rid of Abbott Edward Kirby from Rievaulx?'

I nodded. I had heard the story, but not the detail. And the devil, as they say, was in the detail. He went on: 'Sir Thomas accused Abbot Kirby of mismanaging the affairs of Rievaulx. This was a very serious charge indeed and one which, if it had been found to be true, would have ended Edward Kirby as abbot. Abbots from monasteries in the north were appointed to look into the affairs of Rievaulx. I don't know what the others said, but I could find no fault with Edward Kirby's management and I said so.'

'But if you told the truth Father Abbot, how could any man mark you?'

William Thirsk laughed. 'You are an innocent, my old friend. Thomas Manners wanted to get rid of Edward Kirby because Edward would not play Thomas Cromwell's game. He would not agree,' and here William paused and chose his words with care, 'He did not understand the needs of King and Church in changing times.'

So that was it. The Abbot of Rievaulx had been less than keen to hand his abbey over to the King and so his patron, Thomas Manners, had concocted this charge against him. My own abbot continued: 'And these men, Leyton and Leigh, work for Thomas Cromwell.' He stood up and it was time for me to go. 'Watch your back, Brother Benedict. There are traitors within our gates.'

I worked long into the night, changing a figure here and a sum there. I, alone of all the monks, dealt with the tradesmen and was responsible for our stores and supplies. My second candle was almost burned down when there was a gentle knock at my door. I opened it, and there stood the novice Paul. 'Brother Benedict, may I speak with you?' Another surprise in a day full of them. I held my door open wide and nodded. Paul must have slipped unseen from his dormitory. What could the boy have to say that brought him to my door, pale, frightened, and so unlike the unruly lad who had accosted me earlier in the cloisters?

'Brother Benedict, I know you to be a friend to our abbot, William Thirsk.'

I nodded.

'I have listened where I should not listen and I have heard that which will harm him. I have lain awake, sick with worry. Then I saw your candle burning.'

I nodded again. The boy was close to tears. 'I don't listen to gossip, Paul, but these are dangerous times. Tell me what you heard and then you can leave matters with me and go to your bed in peace.' He looked relieved, but what burden was I taking on? I could do nothing but listen.

'The novice-master sent me on an errand and as I was walking back up the sacristy passage I heard whispering. So, I stopped to listen. One voice said, "So it is settled. Cromwell has taken my six hundred marks and has agreed to my paying one thousand pounds

to the king over the next three years. William Thirsk will be thrown out and I will be abbot." Another voice said, "And will you honour your promise to me and make me Prior?" The first voice replied, "It will be as God wishes. But I can promise you I will do more for Fountains than that old fool Thirsk. Cromwell will eventually close us down. Of that I am sure. But I will get the best arrangement I can for you, for the monks and for myself." Then the monks moved off and I could hear no more. Oh, Brother Benedict, what does it mean? What will become of us?'

I held Paul's shoulders firmly. 'No evil will befall us for we are in God's hands. You have given me the burden of what you heard. Now go to your bed and sleep. But before you do, you must tell me one last thing. Whose voices did you hear?'

Slowly Paul replied, aware of the enormity of what he was saying. 'One of the voices was that of Brother Marmaduke Bradley. The other I do not know but he sings out of tune in the choir.'

What a burden! To know the future and to be powerless to change it.

It all happened as Abbot William Thirsk had guessed. Richard Leyton and Thomas Leigh reported on what they found at Fountains. They said that Abbot Thirsk was a 'fool' and a 'miserable idiot'. They accused him of selling the Abbey's timber and of stealing jewels from the Abbey's treasury. They said that Brother Bradley was 'the wisest monk within England.'

And so it was Abbot Bradley who faced the Visitation, organised by Thomas Cromwell, in November 1539. By this time William Thirsk was dead, hanged at Tyburn for joining the Pilgrimage of Grace which opposed the closing of the smaller monasteries. How he would have hated what happened to Fountains! But Abbott Bradley did well. He may have bought his position, but he fought for us. We all got pensions. The smallest was £5 and the largest nearly £7. The Prior got £8 and Abbot Bradley? Well, he accepted £100 a year.

All that was a long time ago. I am old and ready to die. I think often of those days. But I cannot rid my mind of the two last abbots at Fountains, Thirsk and Bradley. Thirsk, dead on a gibbet at Tyburn, and Bradley, living quietly on his pension until he died in 1553. Did they deserve their fate? To this day I do not know.

Watching Martyrs Burn

Henry VIII and his son, Edward VI, changed England from a Catholic to a Protestant country. When Mary came to the throne in 1553, she began to change England back to being Catholic. During her reign many Protestants were burnt at the stake for refusing to change their faith and become Catholics.

'They are just two old men,' I said to my grandmother. 'Grandmama, they are just two old men! There must be a mistake. Tell the sheriff. He must be burning the wrong people, can't he see that? How can two old men like that be a threat to anyone?'

'Hush, Hughie, my love,' hissed my grandmother. 'They have the right people sure enough. It's not up to us to question their ways.'

My grandmother had brought me to see two Protestant bishops burn at the stake. Given the way people talked about these two men I expected them to be huge and evil-looking, maybe even with devil's horns and tail. I certainly didn't expect them to look like the sort who worked in the university, one of them so old and frail that he could hardly walk.

'We live in troubled times,' my grandmother added, seeing that I was still distressed. 'And if we don't want trouble ourselves, then we need to keep our mouths shut.'

'Right enough, auntie!' said a fat red-faced man next to her. 'All this chopping and changing of religion, it's going so fast we don't know what to think! First it's the Roman religion, then the new religion and now back to the Roman religion again! Change a monarch, change a faith, that's what it seems to be now-a-days! Best keep your feelings to yourself and trust God to sort the whole thing out come Judgment Day, that's what I say!'

'But sir,' I asked, 'why are they burning these old men?'

'Well now, son, I think the Queen'd say it was to save their souls, to get them to change to the "right" religion. But there's people who'd say that she's getting her own back for the time they tried to get her to change her religion, back when her brother was king. Hush, now, the sermon's starting.'

The sermon was quite short and I didn't understand much of it. When it was over Bishop Latimer tried to answer. He was told that they couldn't speak unless they became Catholics first. And even if they did, this wouldn't save them from burning, but it would save their souls. They refused.

Bishop Ridley took off his clothes, all except for his undershirt, and tossed them into the crowd. Then his brother-in-law tied a sack of gunpowder around his neck and one around Bishop Latimer's.

'Why has he done that?' I asked.

'So's it'll catch light with the sparks and explode and help them die quicker. It's a kindness to them,' said the fat man.

Ridley and Latimer climbed up onto the pile of wood to the stake. A soldier then tied them to opposite sides of the stake with a thick chain, which he fastened around their waists. Latimer spoke. Though he was an old man, his voice was steady and clear.

'Be of good cheer, Master Ridley,' he said. 'We shall this day light such a candle by God's grace in England as, I trust, shall never be put out.'

I looked around me. Some people were crying. Certainly there were very few who were cheering, many looked ashamed.

'What does he mean?' I asked.

'He means he believes in his religion,' said my grandmother. 'And that he hopes that by dying bravely they will go to heaven and convince a lot of people that their religion is the right one after all.'

'So which is the right religion?'

'I don't know my love. But I know they do seem to be good brave men.'

'Can't we save them?'

Even as I spoke, the men around the stake lit the wood under Bishop Ridley. The wood caught quickly.

'Oh,' said my grandmother sadly, 'it's good and dry, the wood.'

'Isn't that good? You always say a fire should have dry wood.'

'It's good in a fire at home my love, but not this sort. If it was wet it would make lots of smoke and then they might be knocked out by the fumes before the flames got to them. Some people bribe the guards to water the wood beforehand. Sometimes guards take the money but don't do it.'

From the look of dismay on Bishop Ridley's brother-in-law's face, I think that's what happened.

Bishop Latimer died almost at once, perhaps his heart gave out with the heat. My grandmother said he must have been all of seventy, a great age for any man to live to. But Bishop Ridley suffered horribly.

For weeks after I woke screaming at night from dreams of the heat of the fire, the smell of burning flesh and the screams of the dying man. Until that day I had gone to church unthinking. It was just something the family did on Sunday. From that day about two years ago, I have never set foot inside a church without thinking of Bishops Latimer and Ridley. And now I wonder if their way of worship is the right way. So maybe they lit their candle after all. I wonder how many more people who were in the crowd that day feel the same way I do?

Old Faith, New Faith

The religion of Scotland changed only once, from Catholic to an extreme form of Protestantism. It was a big change. This story is set at a time when the new faith is being imposed on people who are still attached to their old faith.

The tall stranger stood on a large boulder outside the churchyard gates. Dressed from head to foot in black he had a grim face to match. He raised a dark-sleeved arm to quieten the chattering villagers. 'Listen good people of Crail,' he shouted. 'And mind you listen well!'

People were jostling each other, pushing forward, straining to hear. Lizzie clutched Davie's hand, glad to have her brother beside her. They squeezed further forward. Davie was slim and tall for his sixteen years. Lizzie, six years younger, was much shorter. She choked on the stink of fish guts from the skirts and aprons of the fish-wives who had rushed up from the harbour when word of the visitor had reached them. At last they reached the front. Now the voice of the preacher was almost deafening but at least Lizzie could hear what he was saying.

'None shall be saved but by the Word of God! The Catholic Mass is a blasphemy, hear you! Praying to saints is worshipping idols! To believe that they have any power today is superstition. Priests have made themselves rich through the weakness of you, the people! And you...,' he pointed accusingly, glaring meaningfully from one face to another, 'you, good people of Crail, who have so many priests in your church living off your money, you should know!'

The crowd stood in silence. They had heard many travelling preachers in the last few years. They knew well not to agree, or disagree, this early in the sermon.

The preacher went on, 'But no longer! Those days are past now! A new light is dawning on the land! The light of the True Word of God!'

Lizzie felt a shifting in the people around her. She sensed they were not convinced by this argument. But the preacher pushed on. 'Prayer, my good people! Prayer to Almighty God alone! And, most importantly, obedience to the Word of the Holy Bible. These are the only ways to be saved. And you must keep Sunday, the Sabbath Day, holy! You must not buy and sell on the Sabbath, nor do any

kind of work, and that includes fishing!' He looked at the faces below, knowingly.

Lizzie fidgeted. She did not understand Reformers, but they always seemed to be shouting, and they made her nervous. There was a murmuring in the crowd. At last, a brave soul at the back called out, 'But Mister! The people of this town were given a special Royal Charter to let us fish on the Sabbath by no less than King Robert the Bruce himself. He said it was to be for all time.'

The preacher ignored the comment. 'Last year,' he went on, 'Mister Knox himself warned you of the evils of fishing on the Sabbath and yet we hear that you still do this. In the future, woe betide anyone breaking God's Law! Mind, it will not go unnoticed.'

Davie listened grimly. He knew all too well how the Reformers would find out. His stepfather, Walter, had joined the new religion the previous year. He would happily report on the doings of the Catholic Church and the people of Crail.

The preacher jumped down from his boulder, still speaking as he strode forward. 'Each parish has to look after the burden of their sins – the lame, the blind, the poor, the widows and the fatherless.' He reached Lizzie and took her by the hand. 'Come lass!' he commanded in his rough voice, 'Sit ye on the stone.' He lifted her up and sat her on the stone, where all could see her. 'Look long at this little girl, my people,' he bellowed. 'She is blind, as most of you well know. Her blindness is caused by the sins of all of you! So God wants you to care for her. He has placed this burden on you as a constant reminder of your sins! The Word of God in the Holy Bible says so!'

Lizzie slipped down from the boulder and ran, she neither knew nor cared where. She had to get away from the ranting preacher and the angry, shouting crowd, though she had no idea whether they were angry with her or the preacher. Davie raced after her, and caught up with her.

'Oh Davie, Davie!!' Lizzie cried. 'How could he say such things about me? Why did he shout at me so? I hate him! I hate him!'

Davie held her close. What could he say to comfort her? It wasn't possible to tell her to pay no attention to the preacher. Times had been hard at Crail, ever since Mister Knox's sermon the year before. Their lives had been in turmoil with all the new Church reforms, all the new regulations. Even the peace of the school he went to had been affected by the riots and unrest in the town, and the teachers torn between the Old Faith and the Protestant Reformers. Where would it all end?

Adapted from *The Dark Shadow*, by Mary Rhind.

Disasters at the Theatre

At the time when the most famous English playwright, William Shakespeare, wrote his plays, there was only one place in England with permanent theatres for performing plays in – London. The city had several rival theatres, all competing for audiences and for the support of rich people who would pay at least some of their expenses. All the actors were men and boys, with the boys playing the female roles. Scenery, props and costumes were often simple, with thedialogue of the plays being used to inform the audience about the scenery, the characters and even the time of day.

The Armada: First Meeting

This story tells how Giles, an English boy disguised as a Spanish cabin boy, sees the attempted invasion of England by the Armada in 1588 from the Spanish side. England was being attacked partly because of her support for the Dutch against the Spanish. Against the odds the English won.

The great Spanish Armada finally set sail from Corunna on 12 July. One hundred and twenty-five ships and thirty thousand men had set sail from Lisbon in May, but storms had driven them into shore to repair and take on supplies. Even to Giles, an English boy disguised as a Spanish ship's boy on the *San Juan*, the Armada looked strong enough to defeat the English fleet. And if the English navy was beaten this would leave the way clear for the Spanish army stationed in the Netherlands to cross the Channel and attack England's coast.

A young Spanish soldier standing next to Giles on the deck of the *San Juan* looked at the clear blue sky and said, 'This isn't war. It's a holiday jaunt – with all the riches of England as a prize at the end of the journey.'

Giles smiled, then moved away to watch the other soldiers practising for boarding the enemy ships when they closed in. These soldiers also looked confident.

But things weren't going to work out as well as they thought. As they approached the English coast they could see warning beacons burning in a long line east to west, and they began shouting and singing as though they had already landed and conquered England and taken the Queen prisoner. But even before their cheers had died down, the look-out was screaming down through his speaking trumpet, 'Watch out! Watch out! The English are coming in behind us!'

And there they were, the long, low English ships moving in like hounds for the kill, the wind full in their sails, their cannon belching smoke and cannon balls from long range. A Spanish cannoneer close to Giles threw up his hands in dismay. 'We have bigger cannons,' he said, 'but look how far their guns can fire. And they can fire six balls to our one. How can we ever hit them if they stay out of the range of our guns?'

Giles watched the Spanish cannon-balls plopping into the sea short of their targets and put his hand over his mouth to hide his grinning. Then he saw a Spanish galleon hit and explode into a huge ball of flame, settle in the water and sink so fast that even he was horror-stricken. Then another, and another...

The desperate cannoneer cried, 'Thank God they are sheering off. But they will be back again, these English! I know, because I've fought them before, up and down the Spanish Main. Once they've got their teeth into you they never let go. They're like bulldogs, or devils – I don't know which to call them. They are the fiercest fighters in the world, I think, once their cold blood has been warmed!'

The cannoneer was right. Within half-an-hour the wind had changed again and the English were back, blasting as they came. This time their target was the *Santa Cruz*. Giles watched as the smaller, faster, and more deadly English ships darted around the Spanish galleon. She was now cut off from the rest of the Armada and she couldn't manoeuvre fast enough to cope with the enemy. Her guns roared like a thousand lions; her cannon balls churned up the sea all around the speedy English ships. But not a single shot hit the target. Whereas round after round of English shot smashed into the sides of the *Santa Cruz*. But still she didn't sink or explode.

Don Carlos, captain of the *San Juan*, weeping tears of pity and shame that such a fine ship should be so mauled, groaned, 'I have half a mind to go to her aid.'

Suddenly the tattered ensign which fluttered on the mainmast of the *Santa Cruz* vanished as if by magic. The English ships ran alongside, fearless now, their guns silent. Trumpeters blew a victory blast.

'She has surrendered to the English devils!' Don Carlos said, amazed. 'I would rather die than do such a thing. I would put a bullet through my head and be glad to do so.'

Later that day during a lull in the fighting, the news spread among the Spanish that the captain of the *Santa Cruz* had done just this, in full view of the first English boarding party.

Adapted from *Wickham and the Armada*, by Henry Treece.

The Truth about Guy Fawkes?

In 1605, Sergeant Edward Kendal, the executioner from Lancaster Castle, travelled south to London. With him was his son and a girl, Ellie. Ellie had been imprisoned in Lancaster Castle for witchcraft. When King James I wanted to speak to a witch, Ellie was sent for. John and his father were ordered to take her south. When they arrived in London they became involved in a mystery.

4 November 1605

They said that Ellie was evil. But I never saw true evil until I saw the Tower of London that day. Out of the mists of the Thames rose its grim and grey walls. The smell of the pigs kept under the shelter of the walls was sickening. And over everything hung an overwhelming feeling of death. Cruel-beaked ravens stared down from the walls and somewhere within some strange creature roared like the Devil in torment.

The guard at the gatehouse checked my father's documents and sent for the governor. We waited in silence, watching the bustling workmen dragging cartloads of stone and mortar to build new walls. Carpenters were hewing and planing planks of wood. No one looked happy.

The governor walked slowly, stiffly towards us. A tired old man with small eyes that looked sharply down a long nose. A ruff around his neck pushed his square beard upwards and gave him a bristling fierceness. 'I'm Sir William Waad, Lieutenant of the Tower.'

'Sergeant Edward Kendal, Lancaster Castle,' my father said. He didn't introduce me or the girl.

Waad's thick moustache turned up in an imitation of a smile. 'Lancaster. Good. A fine castle,' he said.

'Not so fine as the Tower of London,' my father replied, clearly trying to make a good impression.

Waad began to walk towards the great tower in the centre and my father fell into step with him. 'Don't you believe it, Kendal. When I took over from Sir George Hervey two months ago the place was a shambles. Doors left open everywhere. No control over who visited prisoners, who came or went. I've increased the guards, I'm having new walls built... and more doors closed. People come here to suffer a little, Kendal.'

My father nodded in eager agreement. He knew all about making people suffer. 'No one's escaped from Lancaster in the twenty years that I've been sergeant there,' he said grimly.

Waad stopped and looked at my father carefully. 'I have trouble finding enough good men, Kendal,' he said. 'Honest and trustworthy men. There are dangerous tasks ahead of us and I'd like your help in a little adventure we have planned for tonight.'

10 November 1605

In the days after the arrest of Guy Fawkes, everything – and everyone – changed. My father became accustomed to his new role as warder in the Tower. He began strutting around and giving orders just as he had done back in Lancaster Castle. He made sure I was given a properly paid job as a junior guard – hours of boring duty guarding doors with odd spells of carrying messages for prisoners.

As I guarded Guy Fawkes' cell one afternoon, Ellie brought some food for the prisoner and some extra for me. She sat on a stool opposite me, her thin back pressed against the stone wall. 'How is Mr Fawkes?' she asked.

'Weaker every day,' I said. 'Most days they take him to the dungeons under the White Tower and the Earl of Salisbury or Sir William Waad questions him. I think he's told them very little.'

'He's brave,' she said. 'But the government knows everything about the plot... it's all we talk about in the kitchens! Guy Fawkes was the first one they caught, but it wasn't his plot.'

'It was some Catholic gentleman, wasn't it?' I said. The guards didn't gossip in the way the kitchen staff did but I'd picked up some pieces of the story.

Ellie leaned forward. 'It was someone called Robert Catesby who started it. He'd been fined and imprisoned for being a Roman Catholic so he got together with two friends – Thomas Winter and John Wright – and they plotted to blow up Parliament. They didn't know enough about gunpowder so Thomas Winter went over to the Netherlands and found an old schoolfriend who was an expert.'

'Guy Fawkes,' I nodded.

'That's right. They had a house next to the Parliament buildings and started to dig a tunnel through the walls and under the House of Lords. But they were gentlemen – they weren't used to that sort of work – and they had problems with damp from the river seeping in, so the tunnel was going really badly. They had to bring other people into the plot – some to dig and some with the money to buy the gunpowder. In the end there were thirteen plotters.'

'But they must have got through in the end,' I said.

'No! An amazing thing happened. One day as they were digging they heard a roaring sound above them. It sounded like a river over their heads. They were terrified. Guy Fawkes went to see what it was and found it was coal being piled in the cellar above their heads. That cellar was directly under the Parliament chamber... and it was for rent!'

'So...,' I said slowly, 'they rented the coal cellar?'

'That's right! They paid off the coal merchant and started loading gunpowder into the cellar. It was so easy – and so much drier, of course.'

'My father said the gunpowder barrels were covered with bundles of firewood. The opening of Parliament was put back to the fifth of November, so they had plenty of time to get it all in place. They say there was enough powder there to blow the building up three times over!'

'It's as well it was discovered when it was,' I said.

Ellie leaned forward and looked at me seriously. 'I don't think so, John,' she said. 'I don't think there was ever any chance of James being blown up. The Earl of Salisbury knew about the plot long before the fifth of November!'

I nodded. 'There was that letter to the Roman Catholic Lord Monteagle warning him not to go to Parliament,' I remembered. 'Someone betrayed Guy Fawkes,' I said. 'Who?'

Ellie stood up and brushed crumbs off her thin and shabby dress. 'Why don't I ask him?' she said.

Adapted from *The Truth about Guy Fawkes?*, by Terry Deary.

Bewitched

In 1644, Matthew Hopkins set himself up as the 'witch-finder general' in England. Some vicars invited him in to their parishes to clear them of witches. Others did all they could to keep him out.

When the letter from Matthew Hopkins came, I knew what to do. I went straight down to the church to pray. That's what vicars do when they have a problem. They take it to God. And you usually get an sign of what to do, though it's not always the one you expect. I knelt in front of the altar and put the whole situation to Him. Should I say 'Yes' to Matthew Hopkins, and rid my parish of witches? And would this mean that every old woman who keeps a few herbs and cures a few aches and pains is accused, tortured and maybe hanged? Or do I say 'No' and end up with a parish full of witches and get myself accused of being a witch-lover? There was no answer. I waited. I lit two candles and put fresh rushes on the floor. Then I knelt again and prayed again. Nothing.

Back home, Tom the pig-man was waiting, twisting his cap in his hands and trying to scrape the muck from his boots. Was there a problem with the tithe? Was he – again! – looking to delay giving one-tenth of his piglets and bacon to the church? But it wasn't that. It was something quite different.

'Er, I wanted a word, vicar, about Mother Demdike.' Oh, no. Not again. It all came out in a rush.

'I was driving the pigs along Low Lane to the woods. They grub around there for roots and acorns. We met Mother Demdike, wrapped in that tatty grey cloak, and muttering to herself, as always. Well, you know what pigs are, especially when the piglets are with them. She could have stood aside, in the hedge or ditch, but, no, she keeps on walking. The pigs rushed her and she tripped and fell. She came out of that ditch shouting and swearing and covered in mud. And what words! No good woman would know them, let alone use them. I just walked on, I can tell you. But I felt her eyes on me, boring into the back of my head until the hairs on my neck stood on end. I felt her curse on me and mine. When I got back home, I was in a fair state. But my wife was worse. Petrified she was. Little Dickon was sick. Covered in red spots from head to foot. And those spots came at the time Mother Demdike was crawling out of that stinking ditch. She's a witch, vicar, and it's time she was seen to.'

Yes, well, the children in Northwood have all got the measles. It was only a matter of time before our village caught the infection. More coffins. More little graves in the churchyard. I would have to warn Gethin and get him started digging so that we were ready.

But Tom wasn't finished. 'Don't just listen to me, vicar. I've brought Martha along.' This was beginning to look like a deputation. If only I had been given some sign, back in the church, I would know what to say to Tom and Martha. As it was, I could only listen. Martha's story was simple.

'I was milking, head against my best cow's side, my hands pulling the teats and a good stream of milk going into the bucket. I felt someone looking at me. Still pulling the teats, I turned my head and there she was. Mother Demdike. Just standing there. Looking. You'd think she had never seen a cow being milked before. She didn't say anything and neither did I. When the bucket was full of good, warm, creamy milk she coughed and spat. "Could I have a drink of that milk? My throat's raw and I have no milk at home." Give her some of my best milk? The milk I use to make butter and sometimes cheese? Certainly not. I sent her on her way. "Get off," I shouted, "Get you gone. And if you want milk, go milk your cat!" She went, of course, dragging her lame foot behind her and muttering, always that dreadful muttering. The next day that cow was dead. It's got to stop, vicar. It's got to stop before she bewitches any more living creatures.'

Cows do get sick and animals do die suddenly. Martha wasn't that good at looking after her stock. But was I hearing just a bit too much about Mother Demdike for comfort? I sent Tom and Martha on their way.

I went for a walk. Maybe the air would clear my head and make my decision clear. And there I was, walking past Mother Demdike's cottage. I looked over the wall. She was nowhere in sight. At first, all I saw was a beautiful cottage garden. Then the sun went behind a cloud, the light changed and I saw nothing but horror. There were the aconites, poppies, henbane and foxgloves, which together make an ointment that is said to help witches fly. There were enough deadly nightshade plants, jimsonweed and hellebores to poison the whole of London, let alone our village. The two hawthorn trees were in flower and, of course, hawthorn flowers in the house mean death. And that huge clump of cinquefoil! When cinquefoil is mixed with soot and water parsnip, witches talk to the dead. My gaze wandered up the old oak to a massive clump of mistletoe. We all know that mistletoe is used in spell-casting. Then the sun came out again and the garden looked much like my own.

I had, of course, had the answer to the question I had asked, on my knees, in my church. The answer hadn't been given there in the quiet stillness. It had been given by Tom and Martha and by Mother Demdike's garden. I took up my pen and began to write my reply to Matthew Hopkins' letter.

When Did You Last See Your Father?

During the English Civil War (1642-9) it wasn't safe to be a Royalist family when the Parliamentarians took control.

I may be only eight but I'm not stupid. My nurse and my mother had warned me. They had warned me long before the men, clad in their iron breastplates and helmets, had burst in, terrifying the servants and shouting, shouting, shouting. All that shouting still echoed in my head. 'Meredith, Meredith, where is that Royalist Meredith? Find him! Get him to talk!' The men tore down tapestries and smashed the oak panelling with their pikes. They clattered up the great wooden staircase and into our bedroom and ripped apart the pillows and hangings on our beds. They slithered down the worn stone steps to the kitchens and overturned the barrels of salt fish and the casks of ale. But they didn't find my father in the house. They didn't find him in the stables, either. They didn't find him in the dovecote, in the hen house, or in the dairy. It all happened just as my mother and nurse had said it would.

Now the soldiers have gone. In their place are quiet, determined men with cruel eyes. I know what they want from me. I know that their leader has taken off his hat just to seem friendly. Just to get me to tell. They can't fool me. But I haven't decided what to do. What would my father want me to do? What is my mother willing me to say? What shall I tell? How much shall I tell? The man is leaning forward again, and here again comes the question I haven't answered yet. 'When did you last see your father?'

Into Battle!

This story is set against the background of the English Civil War between the supporters of Parliament (the Parliamentarians or Roundheads) and the supporters of King Charles I (the Royalists or Cavaliers). Simon, the hero of the story, is on the Parliamentarian side.

As the waiting time lengthened, Simon began to notice little things with a crystal sharpness that he had never known before. Small details and oddities never noticed until now, about the backs of the Regiment's officers out in front. The warmth of the sun on the back of his hand as he held the slender painted Standard-lance. The Standard itself, as he looked up at it, billowing against the sky with quick wind-ripples running through it as through standing wheat. Feathery wind-clouds flecked the blue above it, and a buzzard circled and circled on motionless wings.

It was very quiet, up here in this country of rolling downs and shallow vales at the very heart of England. Simon could hear the quietness of it, through the sharp alien sounds of the waiting battle line; a quiet made up of country sounds, familiar and beloved; the mewing of the wheeling buzzard, the soughing of the wind over the hill-crest before him, the distant whit-whit-whit of scythe on wet stone. Somewhere, someone was haymaking. There might be a war in the next field, but a fine day was a fine day, not to be wasted at harvest time.

The quiet was ripped apart by the strident challenge of distant trumpets; and Simon tensed in the saddle, as the scouts appeared, falling back over the crest of the hill. Parliamentary trumpets blared in reply, and next instant the whole of Ireton's Wing had swung forward over the skyline. Drums took up the challenge, and the Foot were moving forward, and the Right Wing with them, up and over the crest. And now for the first time, Simon saw the King's Army. He looked instinctively for the Royal Standard, and did not find it, for the King was with his reserves.

The Royalist Right Wing was already advancing up the near hillside, led by the red-cloaked figure of the Prince himself, and a spearhead of his own wild young Cavalry. Ireton's troops swept down to meet them, and the two wings rolled together with a formless crash that was more a sense of shock than an actual sound; and from both sides rose a shout that spread all down the lines: 'Queen Mary! Queen Mary!' cried the Royalists. 'God our Strength!' answered the New Model men, and the two war cries seemed to beat against each other in the air above the swaying battle line.

Cromwell was holding his Wing in check, while the oncoming Royalist left drew near. Simon watched them, across the valley and coming uphill at a canter, the sun bright on their naked blades, the tossing plumes, the streaming Standards over all. Nearer and nearer yet! Simon's Standard hand was clenched so tightly on the lance that the knuckles shone white as bare bone. Would the order to charge never come? What is he waiting for? – Now! *Now* or it will be too late!

The enemy were half-way up the slope when at last Cromwell loosed Walley's Regiment down against them. The squadrons swung forward at the trot, their ranks curving a little, then straightening again. Simon saw them check to fire their pistols at point-blank range, and then fall on with the sword. Langdale's Horse met them valiantly, and instantly a desperate struggle was in progress, and Walley's reserves were charging down to join it.

Away to the left, a confused roar was swelling and growing ragged with the raggedness that means a running fight. But for Simon there was only the conflict directly below him; and there, the enemy were giving ground! And suddenly, above the ragged musketry and the roar of battle, the trumpets of Fairfax's Horse were yelping.

'Charge!'

'This is it! This is *us!*' The kettle-drums began to roll; Simon touched his heel to Scarlet's flank, and felt the horse gather and slip forward under him as the long ranks quickened into life. 'Oh, God of Battles, strengthen now our arms!' his heart lifted in wild excitement. This was the real thing, the charge that had been practised so often in the meadows at Windsor. He felt his knees touch against those of the men on either side of him, as they moved forward and down at the trot. The ranks curved and grew ragged, then closed again. The ground before the Right Wing was mostly rabbit warren, hummocky and patched with gorse. Gruelling ground to charge on; but Cromwell had known that when the battle line was formed, and trusted them to get through somehow.

So with rolling kettle-drums and wind-whipped Standards, the Right Wing charged home. 'God our Strength!' Simon heard his own voice above the tumult, shouting at the full force of his lungs, as, following Barnaby, he drove straight into the reeling mass of the Royalist Cavalry.

But Walley's charge had done its work, and already the Royalist Wing was crumbling. Now came this new charge, and before it, despite a valiant resistance, they began to fall back. Soon there was no longer a solid battle line, only a chain of skirmishes. Simon found himself and his Standard Escort cleaving into them, with the Troop thundering at Scarlet's heels. 'God our Strength! Follow the Standard!' All around him were battling figures, upreared horses' heads, and a raving, roaring turmoil that seemed to engulf him like a sea. There was a thick mingled smell in his nostrils, of burned powder and blood and sweating horses. He ploughed on holding the Standard aloft, and found, with a vague surprise, that the press was thinning out. The Royalists were falling back faster now. Langdale's Horse was just about finished. Simon ranged up beside Barnaby, who yelled to him, 'Done it, by the Lord Harry!' before they were thrust apart once more.

Extract from *Simon*, by Rosemary Sutcliff.

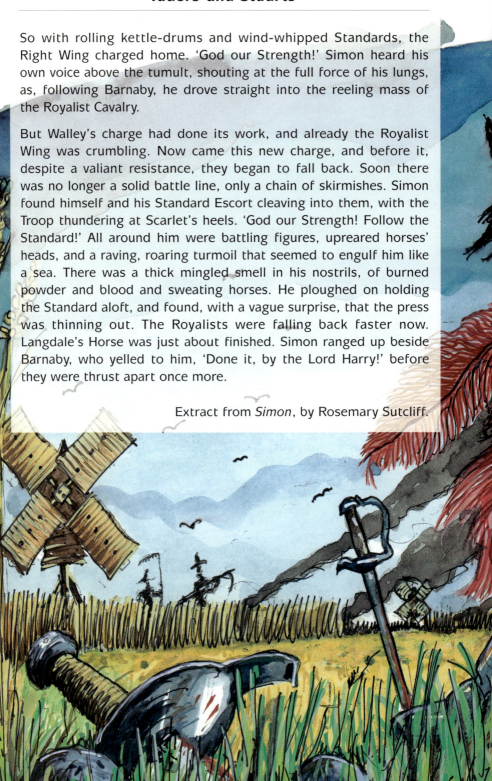

The Grove of Green Holly

In 1651 the future Charles II was being pursued by Oliver Cromwell's men and needed to escape from the country. Two travelling players, Rafe and his grandfather, Gregory Trundle, try to help him escape to France.

The man standing near the shuttered window was immensely tall. He was almost as tall as any man Rafe had ever seen. His hair, cut short, was black, and his skin was swarthy. His mouth suggested he knew well how to laugh, but his clothes were travel stained, his boots dusty and his eyes red with fatigue. Yet looking at him Rafe knew him to be a king and he wondered how he should behave. He looked at his grandfather for instruction. Gregory Trundle advanced as Mr Green – or whatever his true name might be – presented him as 'the actor, sir, who may be able to assist you.' Taking his cue as readily as ever, Gregory contrived a bow merely of the head which seemed to proclaim in one movement recognition, loyalty, silence, respect. So Rafe, too, dropped his chin on to his chest, standing up straight as he did it so that afterwards his grandfather told him he needed little instruction in grace.

'Were you ever of the King's players, Mr Trundle?' the tall man asked.

'No, sir, I was at *The Rose* and *The Globe*, and later had my own travelling company.'

'Then you have often played the king, I daresay.'

'Without vanity, I may say I have done so many times, sir.'

'And truly,' said the man smiling, 'you have the look of some kings. Do you also know how a king should not look and a merchant should?'

'I know this very well, sir.'

'I am somewhat in disgrace in England, Mr Trundle. Will you change my face enough to see me safe aboard Captain Tattersall's brig? Enough, say, to face strangers – or worse should the worst come?'

'You may trust me, sir,' replied Gregory in the low, vibrant voice that made the hairs rise on the nape of Rafe's neck. Mr Green was watching all the time, like some sharp-eyed small animal calculating the possibilities of danger.

'Tell the rest I have decided, Green. Come into the next room, Mr Trundle, and let us get to work.' He looked at Rafe. 'You are not alone.'

'My grandson, sir. My apprentice. I pray you will not object. There are few opportunities nowadays for such a one to learn his trade.'

'He is young, but I rely on him as I rely on you.' He put out his hand to Rafe, then dropped it and slid it awkwardly behind his back. It was as well, for Rafe would have dropped on his knee by instinct – and he was not supposed to know this was the King. Seeing him confused, the tall fugitive moved impulsively towards him, putting an arm across his shoulders and pushing him gently into an inner room. 'Come along, boy. Come into the next room and watch your grandfather carefully. See that he does not make me look too villainous.'

All the time, in the room they had just quitted, there was a coming and going and the sound of men's voices in urgent conversation. Once Mr Green came in, looking a little agitated.

'They say there is a chance of Colonel Morley's men riding this way, sir. The wind is still fresh and the tide has turned. Captain Tattersall urges you to go aboard.'

'When will the ship sail?'

'Between six and seven. You can rest until then.'

'It is a long time. Once I am aboard, until the ship sails, I am a rat in a trap.'

'If they come here they will most certainly ransack the inns,' said Mr Green. 'I must remind you it was a close thing at the head of the river this morning, sir. We may not escape another time with no worse than an exchange of insults.'

There was a roar of laughter at that. 'And they got as good as they gave, I like to think!'

'Tcha!', cried Gregory, grabbing a cloth and dabbing at the great smear that followed the laugh. 'You dare not laugh at such a moment – you will ruin the picture, sir, if you do not hold your head entirely still.'

'How is it going?' He snapped his fingers in Rafe's direction. 'The mirror, if you please.'

Rafe handed him the scrap of looking glass which was all they had found to bring. 'Good God! Is this how an honest merchant looks? Twice as villainous as any gentleman!'

'What am I to say to Tattersall?' insisted Mr Green. 'I must tell him your wishes. He has to give his orders. There is still the crew to be dealt with.'

'Well, I will go aboard, then.' He was still laughing. 'I have great faith in Mr Trundle's transformation. I might walk safely through London, I believe.'

'A little more on the chin,' said Gregory, as Mr Green went off hurriedly before there could be any change of mind. Gregory made a quick stroke or two, then rounded out the edges with the ball of his thumb. 'There. It is done.'

All the swarthiness had gone. A pale man with a sombre expression, a downward twist of the lips and a small scar under one eye, peered at his reflection and nodded in a satisfied way.

'Very good. Very good indeed.' He stood up and moved about the room in a new, slouching fashion. 'But I must not over-act, or I am done for. Mr Trundle, I have to tell you I am low in funds, and what I have must buy me a passage. I ask you to trust me. Indeed, I am to trust you, so we shall be on a footing together.'

Then he turned away as if ending an audience and they knew themselves dismissed. As he went into the outer room there was a cry and a murmur and the now familiar laugh. 'Ah – gentlemen – you think I make a good villain!'

'It is a work of art, sir,' someone cried. Gregory looked at Rafe and winked. 'In fact, it is not the best I have done. I am a little out of practice. Gather up all you can and blow the powder off the table, Rafe. Nothing must remain.'

They worked over the room together, collecting even the fragments of cork that Gregory had burnt at a candle. Long before they had cleared away every speck and packed the things back into their bundle, there was silence in the outer room. It was empty when they passed through it. No one remained to offer any further thanks. They had all vanished, all gone silently down the stairs and away towards the harbour, the waiting boat, the brig leaning a little at anchor but lifting to the increasing tide.

Extract from *The Grove of Green Holly* by Barbara Willard

The Secret

During Oliver Cromwell's reign as Lord Protector of England, Lady Elizabeth Dysart lived a dangerous double life. She openly supported Cromwell and was rumoured to be his mistress. Yet at the same time she was spying for the Royalists. Here, her maid tells the story of a secret journey they made together to France.

My mistress shook me awake. 'Sshh, Alys. Dress quickly and wait for me in the carriage by the side door.' I did as I was bid. Warm dress, dark cloak and some bread, cheese and cold pie from the kitchen. I had done this many times before. We were off to Paris again. But what for? And why now, so soon after the last visit?

The carriage clattered onto the jetty, iron wheels ringing against stone, horses' hooves slipping in the rain. The boat was waiting. Dark sails against a darker sky. My mistress whispering, 'Here is the pass for me and for Alys, my maid. Cast off when you are ready.' A horny hand reached out for mine and helped me down. Ropes slithered into the water.

By the time I had made my mistress comfortable in the small cabin and had stowed the basket of food in a locker, the lights of Rye were just a twinkle behind us and those of France still over the horizon. A shuttered lantern swung from a beam, making shadows leap and dance. Timbers creaked. Waves slapped against the boat's sides as we made good speed across the Channel. And still my mistress, the Lady Elizabeth Dysart, wife to the wealthy Sir Lionel Tollemache, said nothing. But there was a stillness about her that made me afraid. I wanted to ask, but I couldn't. My tongue licked my salty lips but no words came.

Lady Dysart turned to me 'Sleep now, Alys. Much lies ahead and many hard decisions.' I wrapped my cloak around me and pulled the hood over my head. Maybe I would sleep. I drifted. I dreamed. I dreamed of parties, where all was laughter and glitter, dancing and music. In my dream I was a lady, not a lady's maid. I danced as well as anyone and dreamed of a tall man in a long black wig and with lace at his neck and wrists, bowing to me on the stairs and of the blood rushing to my face when I realised that I had brushed past the King with hardly a backward glance. I dreamed of the screaming, 'Dead, dead. They have killed the King!' I woke quickly and pushed the hood back from my face. No, she had not spoken. Not this time. She was staring straight ahead with eyes that were looking beyond the boat and the darkness. I drifted into sleep again and once more I was in the gardens with my lady's children. They were dressed in plain gowns and playing catch with a solemn man in a tall hat. And always, as it is with dreams, there was someone there, just out of reach. Someone I couldn't quite see. Someone who had been there for a long time.

I woke slowly this time. My lady had set out the bread, cheese and cold pie. 'Eat, Alys. We don't know when we will do so again.' I didn't say anything, but a voice inside my head said, 'Or whether we *will* eat again.' I was hungry and, by now, very frightened. I forced down some bread and cheese and my lady had some pie. Suddenly I realised the nausea I felt was for real. I threw off my cloak and rushed for the side.

She was standing now, looking back to England, with the look of someone with something troubling on her mind. Suddenly she turned and gripped my arms. 'He is dying, Alys. The Protector is dying. He lies on his great bed in Hampton Court Palace surrounded by his family. Candles have been lit in all the churches and half the world is praying for him. But we have work to do. We cannot waste time talking to a God who will not listen.' She handed me a packet wrapped in oiled cloth. 'When we tie up at the quay, take this packet. Give it to a man who will be waiting for you in the inn by the fish market. He will be wearing a cloak lined with red silk. He is called Henri and he is expecting you.'

I had to ask. I had to know what I was doing, what risk I was taking. 'Why, madam? What are these papers? What danger am I facing? Will they harm the Protector?'

She turned on me. 'Harm the Protector? Harm the only man I ever loved? Think, you stupid woman. How do I know he is dying? Because he got word to me. My Oliver is dying and I cannot be with him because his loving family is there. His cold, dreary wife, his milk-sop son and that daughter who is more of a man than her brother could ever be.'

'But madam,' I ventured, 'Surely my Lord Richard will rule England if my Lord the Protector dies?'

She turned on me again, and I knew I had gone too far. 'Exactly. Now do as you are told.'

Fire!!

On Sunday 2 September 1666 a fire started in Thomas Farriner's bakehouse in Pudding Lane, near London Bridge, in the City of London. By the Friday, old St Paul's Cathedral, 89 churches and 13,200 houses had burned to the ground.

I'm fourteen and I don't want to die. But I think I'm going to. The top beam, well ablaze, crashes down into the hall chamber. My only way out is blocked. A swooshing thud and half the thatch has collapsed. The swirling, choking smoke reaches up to me, perched high on the king post and hanging on for dear life. My eyes are red and swollen and I am coughing, coughing, coughing. And the smell! I have to do something because if I don't I'll burn for sure.

I lower myself until I am hanging by my hands. The wood is hot and I know I'm going to get blisters on my fingers. I swing my legs backwards and forwards, backwards and forwards. Back bending; back breaking. I'm now swinging well and I try to reach a bay post. At least they are still standing. My first swing doesn't take me far enough. I try again, but I'm blinded by smoke. I manage to hook my feet round the post. Not good enough. On the third try my whole body smacks into the sturdy oak post. I wrap arms and legs round the post and slither down, bare legs scraping against the smouldering wood. The beaten earth floor is hot under my feet. I drop to my knees and then flat onto my stomach.

There's air down here. But how much and for how long? Will the rest of the beams hold? Where is out? Crab-like, I make for where I think the door is. My dress is torn and blackened, my hose long gone. Now the door. I've made it to the door. But what lies outside it? Life… or death in the blazing wreckage of what was London?

Fire!!

The Warming Pan

James II of England became a Catholic and later married the Catholic Mary of Modena. When Mary became pregnant there were fears that a male heir would make England a Catholic country again. This story begins with Mary close to giving birth and calling for her Italian midwife to hurry to England to be with her.

It took three weeks to get to my lady Mary's bedside. I was expected. 'The mistress Francesca to see the Queen! Make way – quickly!' The corridors of St James' Palace rang with the cries of courtiers as I was hurried to the royal bedchamber. Queen! How difficult to think of her as Queen of England. I last saw my lady when she was fifteen, decked in laces and silks, ready to marry James, Duke of York. Now he is King and she Queen of England. And when did I first see her? When I was a young midwife attending her mother. They were my hands that took her from her mother's body, my fingers that cleared the mucus from her mouth, and it was I who held her up and slapped her bottom to make her cry and draw air into her tiny lungs. But enough of that. There will be another birth, here, now. And one that, by all accounts, will not be easy.

The royal bedchamber was full of people. This was a royal birth and an important royal birth. Nothing must go wrong. I turned towards the bed. By the sound of things, the contractions were coming regularly. Suddenly my lady saw me.

'Francesca! At last! Come here to me.'

I crossed to the bed and knelt beside it.

'Listen, Francesca. You must be a witness. This baby will be born alive and healthy. A Catholic prince for England!'

I squeezed her hand as the pain came again. But I wondered. How did she know? Maybe she was simply saying what she hoped for. Maybe. 'Let me examine you, my lady.' I was reaching under the sheets and bedclothes when suddenly a strong hand gripped my wrist.

'That will not be necessary, mistress Francesca. Everything is under control.'

The royal doctor, of course. A man. It was the same in Italy. Gradually men were taking over. We women had been delivering babies since the beginning of time. Now men had decided this was their work.

'If you could wait over there, mistress, until you are needed again.'

He was all smiles and bows and courtesy. Why was I here? Why had I been called half way across Europe? Because my lady had asked for me. To help at the birth or, as she had just said, to be a witness? And a witness to what?

'Aahh! Aahh!' Two agonising screams and I knew there wasn't long to go. Five daughters and a son in fifteen years. And all dead. So many dead babies. My lady deserved better this time. I looked across to the doctor who had stopped me examining her. I could see he was anxious. He couldn't keep still. His hands kept going to his pockets. I knew what he had there. It was one of those new-

fangled leather-covered forceps. One blade in one pocket and one in the other, so as not to frighten the mother. Then, at the first sign of trouble, hands under the sheets, he would whip them out, fit them together and pull the baby out. A perfect delivery! We midwives didn't have a chance. We weren't allowed to handle these forceps, so our births sometimes went wrong. That was how these doctors got their reputations. No one knew they were using instruments. People just believed they were better at delivering babies than we were. Ha!

But what's this? A page opens the door and the Lord Chamberlain's assistant comes in carrying a warming pan. A WARMING PAN!! At a time like this! There must have been some mistake. I took the warming pan from him. The doctor, the one who had stopped me from examining my lady, stepped forward with a look of alarm on his face. 'Give me the warming pan. She has backache. It is quite common in labour. The warmth will help.' Quickly he slipped the warming pan into my lady's bed.

Two deep groaning moans, a long, blood-curdling scream and it was all over. The doctor held aloft a red bawling baby. 'A son! Her Majesty is safely delivered of a Prince!'

Well, now, there's a surprise.

Quickly I went to her. She was lying back on her pillows, pale and serene. She smiled at me. 'There, Francesca, I told you. A healthy son. And you are here to bear witness to that. My own midwife who saw me into this world. Who could be more trustworthy than you? Who, more than you, could be relied on to tell the truth?'

I went back to Italy. I was sent back with courtesy and kindness in a comfortable coach. A month later the payments began. Enough to make my old age comfortable. My reward for being a witness to the truth.

But what was the truth? What had I seen? I saw a woman in bed. I heard the sounds of labour. I saw a warming pan put into the bed. And I saw a healthy baby boy. Of these, I can be certain. But more than that? Did I see the birth of a Catholic prince to the Catholic King James and his wife? Or did I see an unknown baby smuggled into the bed of a woman pretending to be in labour?

Did I see a birth or a deception? That warming pan was certainly heavy.

A Pitiful Cargo

This story takes place in the early days of slave-trading. Here the slaves are African men, women and children, who were kidnapped and sold to English traders. The traders then took them thousands of miles over the sea to the Americas where they were sold as plantation labourers and servants. The story focuses on a young cabin boy's realisation of what the 'cargo' they are taking on is.

I feel as though I'm going mad. I can't shut out the crying and moaning from below decks. I don't know how the rest of the crew can bear it, even for a minute. I feel as though I'm caught up in a living nightmare, which began when we reached the coast of West Africa and from which I can't wake up. If I feel this, I can't even begin to imagine how those poor wretches below deck must feel. The cargo. That's what they're called, all along on the trip – the cargo.

I'd joined as cabin boy on Mr Saverley's ship, out of Bristol, bound for the Americas, to bring back things such as sugar and rum. Nothing was said about Africa until we were underway, but even if it had been, I'd have gone. I knew nothing about this trade, nothing. It was a big adventure, and my first job, my first step on the road to being a man.

The first few weeks I'd plenty to do getting over the seasickness, getting all my jobs done, the worst jobs, the jobs that fall to the cabin boys. I hardly had time to draw breath for conversation. I just said 'Yessir!' a lot and went from one job to the next. Then one day I was being shown how to coil ropes when the sailor teaching me, Ben Watkins, said, 'soon be in sight of land now, boy.'

'Land? I didn't think we would get to the Americas so soon! We must have only done about half our journey! Are you sure, Mister Watkins? I was told we'd be gone a lot longer than this.'

'No, lad, not the Americas. We have to make a stop first. We have to swap our pans and cloth and suchlike for a different cargo. That is how the trade goes. We start from Bristol with one cargo, swap it in Africa for another, then swap that cargo in the Americas for as much rum and sugar and coffee as we can.'

'So what's the new cargo?'

'You'll see lad, soon enough.'

And I did see. We reached the West African coast and anchored as close in as we could get. The captain and the officers went ashore in a boat. They were ashore for several days. While they were gone some of the crew worked below getting the hold ready for the new cargo. It was impossible to see what was going on ashore. All I could see was a beach and some huts at the edge of what looked like a dense forest. At first I watched the shore eagerly, and tried to guess what the cargo would be – something from the trees of the forest, maybe palm oil or some sort of fruit.

Then towards the end of the first week I saw several boats launched from the beach. As the boats drew closer, I heard a strange noise, getting louder, like the crying of gulls, although there were no more gulls about than usual.

'What's that noise?' I asked the nearest sailor.

'First load of the new cargo,' he said. 'Best get ready.' Then he paused and said, 'You have to remember, lad, it's just livestock, cargo, that's all. You'll get used to it. It's just cargo.'

I stood straining to see the boats. Was it animals then? Goats and sheep maybe? Didn't they have enough of them in the Americas? At last I managed to make out the shapes in the boat. It was people! Black African people, like those you see on the streets of Bristol, working as sailors or servants. But these people were all chained together and all naked. And the sound I had heard was their terrified wailing.

They were herded onto the ship and roughly shoved below decks into the hold. I peered through the hatches and could see that they were being forced to lie down, crammed together, head to tail, like pickled fish in a jar. As they were being shoved past me there was a strange smell, and I saw that it came from marks burned onto their shoulders, which were still red and blistered and weeping.

'Will they be alright, like that?' I eventually whispered to one of the younger sailors.

'Some will, some won't,' he replied, uncaringly. 'We reckon to lose about a quarter, if things go well. Course, if sickness breaks out it's the very devil. Could lose half, even more. That really cuts into the profit of the voyage. We have to throw the sick overboard real quick, to stop it spreading.'

A Pitiful Cargo

All kinds of people were herded onto the ship. Men, women, children. Some had very dark skins and heavy features. Others had lighter skins and thinner features. Some were weeping, some were struggling, cursing in a language I did not understand. Others were pleading with the sailors and I thought I could make out different languages among the different sorts of people. Perhaps it would be harder for the sailors to ignore the fact that these were people if only they had been able to speak to the sailors in English. As it was the crew paid no more notice of the pleas and curses than they would to the bleating of sheep. Then something happened that I can still hardly believe.

A young woman was dragged up the ladder to the ship, clutching a baby to her chest. Just as she reached the top of the ladder, she looked around, cried out something in her own language and threw the baby into the sea. She tried to jump in after it, but the sailors were holding her too tightly. She probably knew she wouldn't be able to get away.

How can this be a proper kind of trade? My feelings must have showed on my face, because one of the sailors said what all the others had been saying, 'Cargo, lad. It's just cargo.'

Culloden

The Battle of Culloden in 1745 was fought between the English
and the Jacobite armies on Culloden Moor in the Scottish
Highlands. The Jacobites were retreating to the Highlands, pursued
by the English. Bonnie Prince Charlie's men were starving and
exhausted after months of fighting. The English army were well-
fed and had plenty of fresh soldiers. Some of those fighting on the
English side were Scots who were against the Jacobites. The
English also had cannon, which were deadly when fired across
Culloden's flat moorland at the Jacobites. The battle was fierce and
bloody. An English soldier who was there remembered the scene:
'The moor was covered in blood. Our own men, through killing the
enemy and dabbling their feet in the blood, splashing it about each
other, looked like so many butchers.'

Culloden

The English won. The Duke of Cumberland ordered his men to kill some of the wounded and captured Jacobites. Those left alive were imprisoned, and the wounded were left without medical care. The survivors were later executed or transported. For this the Duke earned himself the nickname 'Butcher Cumberland'.

Before being executed or transported, some of the Jacobite survivors suffered another indignity. They were armed and dressed for battle to pose for this painting of Culloden. The painting presents the battle as one between the Scottish Jacobites and the English redcoats. The Scots who helped the English were conveniently left out. The painting shows soldiers fallen on both sides, but the dominant figure is that of the English redcoat with bayonet raised. There is no doubt who will win.

Charlie is my Darling?

In 1745 Charles Edward Stuart (Bonnie Prince Charlie) led a Jacobite invasion of England. The Jacobites got as far as Derby. Then they turned back for Scotland, pursued by the English army led by the Duke of Cumberland. The Jacobites were defeated at the Battle of Culloden. Bonnie Prince Charlie escaped and became a fugitive.

My nose itches and I mustn't sneeze. Something creeps slowly up my left leg and I must not move. The crooked, jagged half-healed scab stretching between my right elbow and wrist is oozing and itching. I mustn't scratch it. If I move, I will be seen. Flat on my stomach in the peat and with heather almost covering me, I watch. I watch a line of men work steadily up the hillside opposite. They could be beaters raising the grouse. But it's the wrong time of year and their jackets are red. And they're not seeking grouse but a greater prize. They are seeking Charles Edward Stuart. He's not crowned, not proclaimed. But we know him as our rightful king. Idiots! Don't they realise their coats stand out like beacons in a storm? These hills are full of men like me. Watching. Watching these fools. We will watch until they are out of sight, over the shoulder of the hill. Others will take over the watching, and we will report back. We know just where these damned redcoats are and what they are doing. We will never betray our king. He is safe in the Highlands.

It's raining. That slow, misty rain that often falls in the Highlands. It's safe to move now, and I can work my way back down to the bothy. I move quickly down the glen, slipping and sliding where I couldn't stand upright, cushioned by the thick blanket of heather covering the land. Through the mist I see the bothy. I hear voices murmuring. Euan and Archie are there before me. The others won't be far behind. Soon we are all gathered around the smoking fire.

Angus speaks first. 'Word has come from over the glen. Matters move forward and we are asked to help.'

I lean forward. I'm afraid. It's too soon, far too soon. If we move now we'll lose. I can't fight until my scar has healed and my arm is stronger. Others are worse than me. 'It's too soon,' I protest, 'far too soon after the butchery by Cumberland and his redcoats at

Culloden. We need more time for our wounds to heal and then we'll fight again.'

Euan smiles. 'Little brother, you are too impulsive. There will be no fighting the English for many a year. Listen to what Angus says.'

Angus speaks and my heart turns to stone within me. He says that we have reached stalemate. That while the Prince is in the Highlands, the Highlanders will hide him. But all the time the Prince is in the Highlands, the English will search for him. Something has to be done. It has been decided that our cause will be better served if the Prince can get to France. France and Scotland are old allies and the French will support him with men and money. Then, when he has gathered an army he will cross to Scotland, call his loyal Highlanders to his side, and defeat the English in battle.

What a plan! What a disastrous plan! Did we know the French would supply the Prince with men and arms? Did we know how long this would take? Would the Highlanders, goodness knows how many years on, be as ready to die for him as they were now? I didn't say any of this. They're too fired up with plans of defeating the English in some glorious future battle to have any doubts. So, I concentrate on the immediate and the practical.

'But to get to France, the Prince has first to get to Portree on Skye. We all know he is on...' A grimy hand clamps itself over my mouth and an angry voice hisses, 'Never, never say where we know he is. Even if we do. How do you know there's not a redcoat at the door?' I bite the hand sharply. The redcoats were two glens away by now and Dougal is being just a touch too dramatic.

I continue. 'Let me put it straight to you. How is the Prince going to get across to Portree to find a boat and someone to row him to a ship to take him to France?'

Euan looks uneasy. 'It's planned. He'll make his way to the coast where there will be a boat waiting with a rower.'

'Who, Euan, who will be foolhardy enough to row to Skye, to cross the Minch, in this weather?'

Euan looks even more unhappy. 'Flora,' he said. 'Flora MacDonald.'

I have heard everything now. A girl? A GIRL? They were going to trust our Prince and the future of Scotland to a GIRL of not more than five and twenty?

Before I can open my mouth, Euan goes on. 'She's a good choice. She's intelligent. She was educated in Edinburgh and knows a thing or two. If she's caught, she'll give the English a run for their money. She knows how to turn a word and her English is as good as her Gaelic. But she has another advantage. Her stepfather is in charge of the militia on Uist. He'll give her a pass to cross to Portree. No one will challenge her.'

We are lying, side by side, under a clump of ragged hawthorn trees. Below us is a cluster of small, grey fishermen's cottages. We are waiting for our Prince to appear from the third cottage on the left. We are watching for the redcoats. Euan has spotted people moving about on the jetty. He grabs his spy-glass. 'There, there

they go. Three of them getting into the fishing boat.' Then silence, and then some grunting and cursing. Euan had seen two women. Flora was one, for sure. The other was her maid, Betty Burke, and the third was a manservant. The Prince must be hiding somewhere behind Benbecula, unable to get down to the sea. There must be a platoon of redcoats between him and the coast. But I hadn't seen them. Neither had Euan, for all his cleverness and skill at stalking.

I snatch the spy-glass from him. I can see the boat clearly now. It's moving faster as it leaves the tiny harbour for the open sea. I move the glass to the maid. At that moment she turns and looks straight at me. I could have sworn she winked. For that was no maid. That was the bonnie Prince, dressed in women's clothes. I watch until the boat has gone from view. Then I tell Euan. He shouts at me and throws a punch, and there we are, like bairns again, rolling and punching and shouting with relief. For he will be back. The Prince will be back and we will fight the accursed English. This time we will win.

The Sound of Coaches

One stormy December night a coach came thundering down the long hill outside Dorking heading for its overnight stop at the Red Lion Inn. It was *The Flying Cradle* **making its usual journey between Chichester and London. But something unusual happened that night at the Inn. One of the passengers gave birth to a child and then died.**

Who was she? Where had she come from – the dead young woman on the bed upstairs? Her baggage consisted of a bundle of underclothing and a brass-cornered barber's box, but there was nothing in them to give any clues as to who she was. Her black gown, which had been laid neatly across the end of her bed, told nothing. The women said it was of good quality, but pointed out where it was worn almost threadbare in several places. Her shoes, too, had once been smart but were now battered and worn, like her well-mended stockings.

The travellers gathered in the parlour wondered where she had been so desperate to get to that she'd risk making such a journey in her condition? God knew! She'd boarded at Arundel and paid her money for London, and that was that. To her home, maybe? The coachman didn't think so. Her voice had been from the country. She'd never come from London.

'Then to find her lover, maybe?'

The coachman shrugged his shoulders; he was not a man given to ideas.

'What's to be done?'
'The parish will bury her.'
'And her baby?'
'The parish will provide.'

A silence fell on the parlour, and the melancholy sound of the sign banging outside chilled everyone. The candles seemed to shrink and their light fade.

The women were in the kitchen where the baby was asleep by the fire. No more had been seen of it as it had been carried down the stairs than a pathetic tuft of black hair poking out of a shawl.

Could it have dreams already? Disturbing thought. Were its mother's shrieks still echoing in its ears, even as they seemed to be echoing in the wind outside?

'The parish will provide.'

'I… I would like,' said the one of the travellers awkwardly, 'to leave a little money with you, landlord, for the – the baby's future.'

'I'll add to that!' came an abrupt voice from a corner of the room.

'And I!'

'I will, too!'

'I'll spare a copper or two.'

The gloom vanished. Everyone was smiling and laughing and talking at once. Think of it! There they all were – men of business, professional men and humble working men – all united in love and charity for… for a perfect stranger!

'What day is today, landlord?'

'December eighteen.'

'His birthday! Let the four of us who knew his mother send a present every year.'

'We'll send the gifts to you, landlord.'

'No call for that. Send 'em to me.' It was the coachman who spoke. Until that moment he'd remained silent and, to all intents, disapproving.

'Why's that, coachman?'

'His mother paid her fare right through to London,' said the coachman, 'so the tiddly 'un is rightfully owed the rest of the journey.' His voice took on an aggressive edge. 'Stands to reason he can't take advantage of it now, so me and my good lady will shoulder him, as the saying goes, till he's able. It ain't charity, like yours; it's no more than lawful trading.'

The four travellers blinked. They were taken aback. For the first time they saw the coachman and his guard as something other than the furniture of the journey. And a very remarkable pair they were. Though weathered, stern, and sharp with the gun, the guard of *The Flying Cradle* was certainly female. She and her coachman were partners on more than the road; they were man and wife. When the travellers thought of the baby in the kitchen, they couldn't help wondering whether the parish might not have been the kinder choice.

The four travellers insisted on waiting until the body was removed. Silently they stood at the foot of the stairs as the undertaker's men arrived with the coffin and took it to the bedroom to place the body in it.

The coachman and his wife had alreay entered the bedroom. 'Look carefully,' said the coachman quietly. 'Look at her face; look at her hands and fingernails. Look at the colour of her hair and, if you can stomach it, look in her eyes. Look at her lips and remember the smile on 'em. For what you see now is all the little one will have. So make no mistakes. He'll ask, you may be sure. He'll want to know. And you must tell him, adding nothing and taking nothing away. Every detail, Mrs C. Whatever lies there of his mother is in your keeping.'

As the coffin was carried downstairs the travellers bowed their heads.

'Watch it, there...' The coffin jolted and cracked a bannister. The coachman stared at the damage as if that, too, was to be remembered. Then the little party followed the coffin outside into the cold, grey morning and watched it being laid on the undertaker's cart.

'May she rest in peace.'

'Amen... amen.'

From the kitchen came the sound of the baby, crying. 'He knows,' said one of the travellers softly.

'What about his inheritance?'

'Won't touch a penny of it. Forty-seven pounds four shillings, including what was in the poor soul's purse. You were very generous, gentlemen. If his mother had lived, I doubt whether the little one would have done half so well. It's an ill wind, as they say.'

'And that box?' said another traveller. 'I happen to know she'd set great store by it.'

'Oh, yes, the box. A very queer thing for a young woman to be travelling with.'

'Belonged to the baby's father,' said the coachman's wife, abruptly. 'She told me, almost with her last breath. "His father's," she said. "Keep it for him, please." What sort of a man could he have been to leave such a keepsake? An old barber's box with nothing in it but a cheap pewter ring and a pistol.'

Adapted from *The Sound of Coaches*, by Leon Garfield.

The Highwayman

**In the eighteenth century, highwaymen held up stage
coaches and robbed the travellers. If they were caught,
they were tried, and if found guilty, they were hanged.
This highwayman was, perhaps, different.**

The wind was a torrent of darkness among the gusty trees.
The moon was a ghostly galleon tossed upon cloudy seas.
The road was a ribbon of moonlight over the purple moor,
And the highwayman came riding –
Riding – riding –
The highwayman came riding, up to the old inn door.

He'd a French cocked-hat on his forehead, a bunch of lace at his
chin,
A coat of the claret velvet, and breeches of brown doe-skin.
They fitted with never a wrinkle. His boots were up to the thigh.
And he rode with a jewelled twinkle,
His pistol butt a-twinkle,
His rapier hilt a-twinkle, under the jewelled sky.

Over the cobbles he clattered and clashed in the dark inn-yard,
And he tapped with his whip on the shutters, but all was locked
        and barred.
He whistled a tune to the window, and who should be waiting
        there
But the landlord's black-eyed daughter,
Bess, the landlord's daughter,
Plaiting a dark red love-knot into her long black hair.

'One kiss, my bonny sweetheart, I'm after a prize tonight,
But I shall be back with the yellow gold before the morning light;
Yet, if they press me sharply, and harry me through the day,
Then look for me by moonlight,
Watch for me by moonlight,
I'll come to thee by moonlight, though hell should bar the way.'

He did not come in the dawning. He did not come at noon;
And out of the tawny sunset, before the rise of the moon,
When the road was a gypsy's ribbon, looping the purple moor,
A red-coat troop came marching –
Marching – marching –
King George's men came marching, up to the old inn door.

They said no word to the landlord. They drank his ale instead.
But they gagged his daughter, and bound her, to the foot of her
        narrow bed.
Two of them knelt at her casement, with muskets at their side!
There was death at every window;
And hell at one dark window;
For Bess could see, through her casement, the road that he
        would ride.

They had tied her up to attention, with many a sniggering jest.
They had bound a musket beside her, with the muzzle beneath
        her breast!
'Now keep good watch!' and they kissed her.

She twisted her hands behind her; but all the knots held good!
She writhed her hands till her fingers were wet with sweat or
        blood!
They stretched and strained in the darkness, and the hours
        crawled by like years,
Till, now, on the stroke of midnight,
Cold, on the stroke of midnight,
The tip of one finger touched it! The trigger at least was hers!

Tlot-tlot, in the frosty silence! Tlot-tlot, in the echoing night!
Nearer he came and nearer. Her face was like a light.
Her eyes grew wide for a moment; she drew one last, deep
        breath,
Then her finger moved in the moonlight,
Shattered her breast in the moonlight and warned him with her
        death.

He turned. He spurred to the west, he did not know who stood
Bowed, with her head o'er the musket, drenched with her own
        blood!
Not till the dawn he heard it, and his face grew grey to hear
How Bess, the landlord's daughter,
The landlord's black-eyed daughter,
Had watched for her love in the moonlight, and died in the
        darkness there.

Back, he spurred like a madman, shouting a curse to the sky,
With the white road smoking behind him and his rapier
    brandished high.
Blood-red were his spurs in the golden noon; wine-red was his
    velvet coat;
When they shot him down on the highway.
Down like a dog on the highway,
And he lay in his blood on the highway, with the bunch of lace at
his throat.

And still of a winter's night, they say, when the wind is in the
    trees,
When the moon is a ghostly galleon tossed upon cloudy seas,
When the road is a ribbon of moonlight over the purple moor,
A highwayman comes riding –
Riding – riding –
A highwayman comes riding, up to the old inn door.

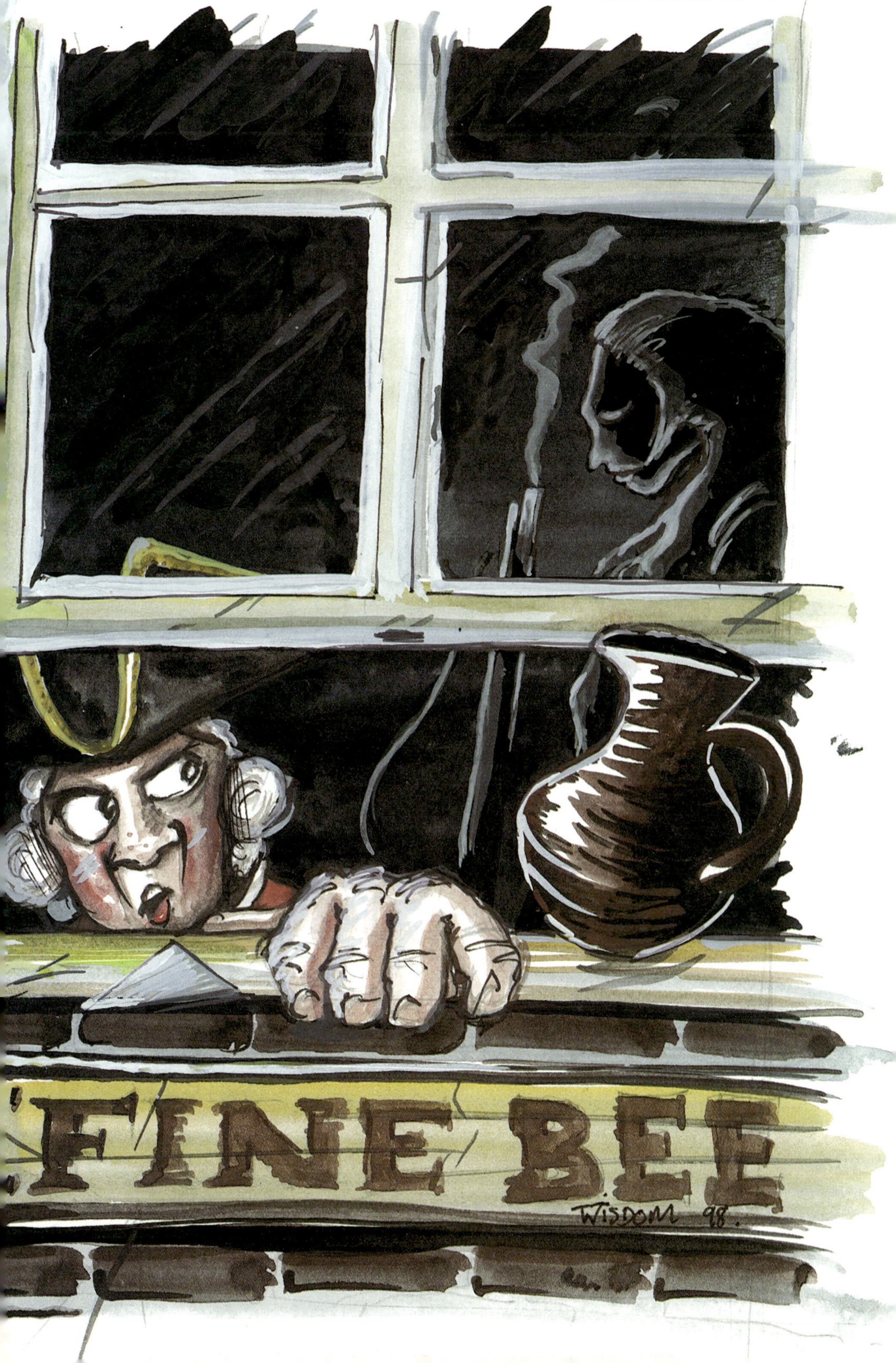
FINE BEE
WISDOM 98.

Over the cobbles he clatters and clangs in the dark inn-yard.
And he taps with his whip on the shutters, but all is locked and
     barred.
He whistles a tune to the window, and who should be waiting
     there
But the landlord's black-eyed daughter,
Bess, the landlord's daughter,
Plaiting a dark red love-knot into her long black hair.

The Highwayman, by Alfred Noyes.